CONTENTS

ONLY THE BEST: CREDITS

Publisher and Editor in Chief	Alexander Kyrtsis
Editor	Veti Nikolopoulou
Travel Research	Alexander Kyrtsis
Text and Historical Research	Nikos Faroupos
Translation	Diana Farr Louis
Photographs	Tolis Zaharakis
Proofreading	Doolie Sloman
Advertising and Public Relations	Viki Magoulioti
Sales	George Gerokonstantis
Accounts	Kostas Moukas
	Dimitris Draïnas
Communications Departament	Panagiota Georgala
Research Department	Faye Nikolopoulou
Secretariat	Athena Serli
	Georgina Karnesi
Logistics	Dimitris Athanasopoulos
Design and Layout	PCR Polgrama Creative Services
Cover Design and Production	EPIPHANIA S.A.
Graphics Consultant	Antony Psychas
Maps	EMVELIA

First Edition May 2001

COPYRIGHT © 2001, AXON PUBLICATIONS S.A.

52 Aigialias Street, 151 25 Maroussi, Greece, tel. (01) 6856093, fax 6856095

email: axon@hol.gr

www. greeceonlythebest.gr

ISBN: 960-377-042-6

SPECIAL THANKS TO:

Father Konstantinos Kylis, Council of Prelates of Naxos, Manos Korres, Dimitris Lianos, Giannis
Margaritis, Christina Agriantoni, Eleftherios Primikyrios, Stuart Thorpe, Michalis Frankiskos,
Yiorgos Haralambopoulos and Vasiliki Hatzopoulou.

NOBODY'S PERFECT

The publisher and authors of **ONLY THE BEST** cannot accept any responsibility for consequences
resulting from the use of this guide. They have made every possible effort to ensure that the information contained in this guidebook was correct at the time of publication. However, while remaining as
objective as possible, they were obliged to make some very difficult decisions in their evaluations
and star ratings.

IMPARTIALITY

In order to ensure the impartiality of **ONLY THE BEST** guidebooks, we do not print advertisements
for hotels and restaurants nor accept discounts or any other return for favourable comments.

YOU CAN HELP US KEEP UP TO DATE

Since things are always changing − prices, renovations of premises, chefs, departure schedules −
we would be grateful for your contributions if you think any revisions are in order. We can be
reached by phone, post, fax or email. The best contributions will be mentioned in our next edition.
Subtantial updates will be rewarded with a free copy of the book.

NAXOS
IN GENERAL

BEST's OPINION

In the 1970s and 80s the island attracted the young who used to camp on the long beach of Agia Anna. Nowadays, however, it seems to have shifted its focus to family tourism. Naxos offers a wide choice of places to stay, entertainment and food, at accessible prices. It also possesses a unique natural beauty, picturesque mountain villages and seaside resorts rimming endless stretches of beach, some of which rank among the loveliest in Greece.

Facilities for tourists are concentrated in Hora and to the south, from Agios Georgios to Agios Prokopis along the southwest coast and from Agia Anna to Agiassos. Sadly, in some of these areas the rush to build hotels and rooms has occurred without regard for the necessary infrastructure or for traditional architecture.

Naxos's size has permitted the dispersal of tourism, making it possible for the visitor to find peace and quiet even during the high season, with the exception of Hora and its immediate vicinity. Nevertheless, anyone intending a July or August holiday should reserve their room well in advance. Time should also be set aside for day trips to the inland villages of the Tragea, many of which are well worth exploring for their dramatic scenery, archaeological sites, Byzantine monasteries and churches, Venetian fortified mansions and castles. Easily reached by sea and air, the island also has a comprehensive network of good roads, most of which are paved, as well as old footpaths interlinking villages and interesting landmarks.

BEST 10: SIGHTS AND ACTIVITIES

NAXOS IN BRIEF

THE NAME
Initially, the island was called *Dias* (Zeus), *Strongyle* (Round) and *Dionysias*. It took its present name from Naxos, the leader of the Carians who eventually settled there.

SIZE AND LOCATION
Naxos is the largest of the Cyclades group of islands and the tenth largest in Greece. It has a length of 30 km and a width of 20 km. Its distance from Piraeus is 104 n. mi and from Rafina 87 n. mi. It lies east of Paros and south of Mykonos and Delos.

POPULATION
Of its approximately 17,000 inhabitants, some 6,000 live in Hora. The second largest settlement is Filoti with about 1,700 residents, followed by Apeiranthos, Koronos, Agios Arsenios and Tripodes (Vivlos), each with populations of about 900, while several villages such as Melanes and Sangri number as many as 300 to 400 inhabitants. As for the new coastal resorts, they rarely boast more than 100 Naxians in summer; in winter they are deserted.

NATURE AND CLIMATE
The island has a very varied landscape: barren, rocky districts, high mountains (dominated by the highest peak in the Cyclades, Mount Zeus or Zas, alt. 1000 m), lush ravines and green plateaus. In the fertile valleys of the hinterland and the west coast where there is water in abundance, the island's main products — potatoes, fruit and olives for oil — are grown. Stock farms are also widespread and Naxos is known for its excellent cheeses, meat and sausages.

The southwest is blessed with many capes and bays lined with broad sandy beaches, while the north coast is carved into coves with smaller beaches. The beaches to the east are fewer but still interesting.

The island also has considerable mineral wealth, such as the marble known from antiquity, granite and emery.

The climate is dry, with mild winters and summers cooled by the northerly wind *(meltemi)* that blows through the Aegean during the hottest months.

THE NAXIANS AND THEIR OCCUPATIONS

Thanks to the island's bountiful agricultural and stock breeding potential, the Naxians did not turn to the sea for their livelihood as did most of their neighbours on the other Cyclades. Thus, there are relatively few fishermen and seamen among them. Nevertheless, many Naxians from the poorer, barren mountain regions were forced to emigrate to Athens or abroad in order to survive. In antiquity the Naxians were superlative sculptors, marble workers and potters; today they are often skilled musicians with a long heritage. Few people are aware that most of Greece's favourite Aegean folksongs were composed by noted Naxians, such as the Konitopoulaios family.

In recent years, as the island's importance as a holiday destination grows, many of its inhabitants have entered the tourist professions.

ARCHITECTURE

The houses of Naxos can be divided into four main categories: the spare stone mansions of the Venetians in the Kastro, with their stern fortress-like character; the merchants' homes outside its precincts, less severe and more luxurious, with marble ornamentation on the façades and wooden decoration in the interiors; the vernacular houses in Hora and in the villages, simple edifices composed of one large room or more complex, with various spaces such as lofts and cellars, often embellished with arches; and finally the Venetian tower-houses *(pyrgi)*. These last are usually imposing structures built for defensive purposes and only rarely incorporate the comforts of a real country manor. The stairs in all the houses are made of stone and very steep, to economize on space. The roofs are almost always flat with a gentle slope to guide rainwater into the cistern and a low ledge round the periphery.

MYTHOLOGY

According to myth, Zeus grew up on Naxos and from there set out to conquer Olympus. He is not the only god with close links to the island. Other deities associated with it are Dionysos, Demeter, Persephone and the giant Ephialtes. In honour of Zeus of Milosios the islanders erected a shrine on Mt. Zas (Zeus), which took its name from the father of the gods.

Zeus fell in love with Semele, the daughter of Cadmus, king of Thebes, and from their union was born (or rather taken from the thigh of Zeus) the wine god Dionysos, who later made sure that Naxos was planted with lots of vines.

The hero Theseus also passed through Naxos, after having slain the Minotaur on Crete with the help of Minos's daughter Ariadne, who gave him the thread to guide him out of the labyrinth. Theseus however abandoned Ariadne on Naxos (there are many versions as to his reasons) and she, according to one legend at least, married Dionysos while he was on the island teaching the Naxians how to make wine. Even today the locals organize wine festivals in honour of Dionysos and Ariadne.

The myth symbolizes the decline of Minoan influence in the Aegean.

7

HISTORICAL OUTLINE

PREHISTORY Thracians and Pelasgians first settlers. Carians, Phoenicians and Cretans follow. Naxos a major centre of Cycladic civilization.	4000-1000 BC
GEOMETRIC ERA Ionians of Attica colonize the island. A period of growth, power and wealth begins.	1000-700 BC
ARCHAIC ERA Naxos governed by aristocrats. Lavish donations made to sacred isle of Delos.	700-480 BC
CLASSICAL ERA Naxians fight alongside other Greeks against the Persians. Naxos joins lst Athenian Confederacy (479-466 BC).	480-320 BC
HELLENISTIC ERA Ruled successively by Macedonians, Ptolemies of Egypt, Rhodians.	320-41 BC
ROMAN DOMINATION Naxos a province of Rhodes. Saracen pirate raids.	41 BC-324 AD
BYZANTIUM Byzantines erect many fortresses and churches. Pirate raids continue without interruption.	324-1207
FRANKS-VENETIANS Marco Sanudo of Venice takes over the island in 1207, builds the formidable fortress in Hora and founds the Duchy of the Archipelago. Venetians rule the Cyclades for more than 350 years.	1207-1564
OTTOMAN OCCUPATION The Turks govern without a break except for four years of Russian rule (1770-74). Collecting taxes is their main preoccupation.	1564-1821
GREEK WAR OF INDEPENDENCE Naxians join in the Revolution of 1821. In 1830 it and the other Cyclades are united into the new Greek state.	1821-1828
MODERN ERA After millennia of farming and raising livestock the Naxians turn to tourism in the 1970s.	1829 to date

HISTORY

PREHISTORY

Naxos was one of the most important centres of the oldest civilization in Europe, the early Cycladic (4000-1100 BC). Archaeologists have unearthed many notable examples of that quintessential Cycladic art form, the spare **marble figurine/idol**. The first people to inhabit the island were Thracians and Pelasgians; they were followed by Carians, Phoenicians and Minoan Cretans. In the second millennium BC, Naxos constituted a bridge enabling the spread of Mycenaean power in the Aegean, as demonstrated by finds from their settlements at **Grotta**, near Hora, **Panormos**, on the southeast coast, and the Mycenaean acropolis at **Kastraki**.

Later, tribes from Ionia (Anatolia) who had settled in Attica sent colonists to the island, introducing an era of widespread growth, during the course of which the Naxians acquired wealth and power and before long set out to found colonies of their own, such as Naxos on Sicily (734 BC). The islanders' greatest threat came from the Milesians of Asia Minor, and they met in battle on numerous occasions. Relations with their neighbours on Paros were also far from friendly; in one confrontation the celebrated Parian lyric poet, Archilochos, was among the fallen.

ARCHAIC ERA

Amongst the dedicatory offerings to the sacred island of Delos there are many displaying the wealth and cultural eminence of Naxos during this period. Examples include the famous **Lions**, the huge (8 m) **marble Apollo of Naxos**, the splendid **House of the Naxians** and others. Other Naxian offerings are the wonderful **Sphinx** at Delphi and the **Artemis of Nikandros**, given to Delos but now in the National Archaeological Museum in Athens.

At this time the island was an oligarchy, governed by nobles called *pacheis*. In 524 BC the tyrant of Naxos **Lygdames** chose the islet of Palatia at the entrance to the main harbour as the site for what he intended as the largest, most magnificent edifice in the Greek world, a temple to Apollo. It was apparently never completed, since he was overthrown a year later in a war with Samos, and of that ambitious scheme only the entrance gate has remained, the monumental **Portara**.

In 506 BC the Naxians withstood the four-month siege by the tyrant of Miletus, **Aristagoras**.

CLASSICAL ERA

In 490 BC the Persian fleet attacked the island, wreaking havoc, burning towns and sanctuaries and enslaving the population. The Naxians found the courage to resist and to fight on the side of the Greeks at the historic battles of **Salamis** and **Plataea**. However, Naxos was never able to regain its formidable power. In 479 BC the island joined the **First Athenian Confederacy**, but thirteen years later it withdrew. Succeeding years saw Naxos again subject to Athenian rule, which shifted after the **Peloponnesian War** to the victorious Spartans.

HELLENISTIC ERA

Macedonian supremacy was followed by that of the heirs of Alexander the Great, the Ptolemies of Egypt, and then of the Rhodians until 41 BC.

ROMAN DOMINATION

In 41 BC Naxos became a province of the new power rising in the West, Rome. The Romans often used the island, as well as others in the Aegean, as a place of exile. In later centuries Saracen pirates, who tyrannized the Aegean, raided Naxos on many occasions. Christianity came early to the island (in the 1st c.) brought by **St. John the Divine** who had composed the Revelation on Patmos.

BYZANTIUM

Naxos was initially subject to the Church of Rhodes, although later (1083) it became itself the seat of the metropolitan (similar to a bishop) for Paros and Naxos. The Byzantines favoured the island because of its fertile soils and strategic location and erected a number of fortresses there. During their rule they built some 500 structures, from Early Christian basilicas and chapels to large fortified monasteries. Many of these still dot the countryside.

FRANKS-VENETIANS

In 1207 the ships belonging to the Venetian noble **Marco Sanudo** sailed into Naxos. Genoese pirates who had taken over the island barricaded themselves into the Byzantine castle of Apalyros and mounted a fierce resistance for 45 days. Sanudo in turn burned his ships, giving his men no choice but to fight until they captured the castle, which they eventually did. In addition to Naxos, the Venetians also took seventeen other islands in the Aegean. Sanudo constructed the stout-walled Kastro at Hora and with the permission of the new Latin emperor at Constantinople founded the **Duchy of the Archipelago**. His successors were able to rule the Cyclades from the Kastro for another 300 years.

Like virtually every other Greek island, Naxos suffered terribly from the catastrophic raid by the Ottoman admiral Khaireddin Barbarossa in 1537, whose corsairs slaughtered, pillaged and enslaved until hardly a Naxian remained.

OTTOMAN OCCUPATION

In 1564 the island was obliged to recognize the supremacy of the Ottoman Turks, who at first contented themselves with collecting taxes and left the administration to the local notables. At that time the Aegean was at the mercy of pirates both from the Barbary coast and free-roaming Christian Europeans, intent on getting a share

Kalavros Tower

of Turkish wealth, which was another reason why the Turks were reluctant to settle on the islands.

The Naxians rebelled several times against both Frankish and Ottoman conquerors to no avail. Turkish rule was interrupted only once, from 1770 to 1774, by the Russians.

GREEK WAR OF INDEPENDENCE

The Naxians were quick to join in the fight to overthrow the Turks when revolution was declared in 1821. With the signing of the protocol of 1830, Naxos and the other Cyclades were incorporated into the new Greek state.

MODERN ERA

The island gradually shook off the habits of centuries of feudalism. But in the process many islanders were obliged to seek their fortunes in Athens or abroad. In the past three decades Naxos has been rapidly developing into a popular tourist destination.

BEST SIGHTS

STEP BY STEP

For your convenience we have separated the island's principal sights into five main regions: **Hora (Naxos Town), Apeiranthos and vicinity, the villages of the interior** with their rich ancient, Byzantine and Venetian heritage, the **north and northeast quarter** with its villages, landmarks and beaches and, finally, the **summer resorts of the southwest coast** and their superb beaches.

Bear in mind that the restored Venetian tower-houses described below are usually open to the public only in August when their owners are in residence.

Apeiranthos

❶ HORA

Χώρα / Hóra

The capital and port of Naxos, Hora has grown up around the large ©©© **Venetian kastro** at the top of the hill above the waterfront. The island's trademark, the ©© **Portara** or enormous doorway of the Archaic (6th c. BC) temple of Apollo, stands on **Palatia islet** facing Delos. It is connected to the larger island by a long narrow causeway constructed to protect the harbour. The temple is thought to have remained unfinished owing to a war between Naxos and Samos.

Most of the activity is concentrated on the waterfront or *perantzada*, which is closed to traffic. Its southern end is chock-a-block with cafes, tavernas, ouzeris and little bars.

Behind the waterfront, the ©© **Old Town** invites exploration; its intriguing vaulted alleyways conceal a variety of shops, bars, tavernas and lovely houses. Several of the steep lanes lead to the medieval Kastro, while others are cul-de-sacs originally aimed at misleading pirates.

The ©**Cathedral (church of Zoodohos Pigi)** was built in the 18th c. on © **Metropolis square** in the Old Town. It contains one of Greece's most beautiful icon screens, noteworthy icons, a carved epitaphios (bier used in Good Friday processions), as well as elements from ancient buildings, for example the columns supporting the dome, said to have been brought from the temple of Apollo on Delos. The archaeological site on the square in front of the Cathedral, between four churches, is a **subterranean museum** with remains of the walls, agora, tombs and workshops of Mycenaean Naxos (**1400-1100** BC).

View to Portara

Cathedral (church of Zoodohos Pigi)

In the shallow water offshore at **Grotta**, which took its name from the caves found at Aplomata, north of the port, swimmers with masks can examine vestiges of what was once an important **Mycenaean city**.

Of the Hora's churches, also worth a look, are the picturesque chapel of ⑥ **Panagia Myrtidiotissa** (early 17th c.), on the tip of the second islet in the harbour, and ⑥ **Agia Kyriaki**, which was a monastery during Ottoman rule.

⑥ ⑥ ⑥ THE KASTRO

Paraporti

Κάστρο Χώρας / Kástro Hóras
Enter through the south gate, the ⑥ **Paraporti**, or the ⑥ **Trani Gate** to the north, with its old wooden door which leads to the main square on the hilltop. Next to the Trani Gate is the only tower that has survived the Castle's original 12; this is the cylindrical ⑥ ⑥ **Crispi tower**, named for the last dukes of Naxos. It is also called the **Glezos tower** after the last owners who donated it to the state for restoration and eventual conversion into a Byzantine museum.

As you climb up the alleys with their smooth flagstones you'll come across several palatial medieval houses with the coats of arms of the Venetian nobles who governed the island from the 13th to 16th c. embossed upon their walls, and every now and then a tantalizing glimpse of the Aegean and farflung islands.

Many of the town's most important buildings are located around **Prandouna square** at the top of the Kastro. Here you'll see part of Marco Sanudo's fortified ⑥ ⑥ **palace**, the five-aisled ⑥ **Catholic Cathedral** (13th c.) dedicated to the Virgin Ypapanti or Gantlema, the ⑥ **monastery-school of the Ursulines** (Kazatza Chapel), the **Capuchin monastery** whose monks serve St. Anthony, the **Franciscan monastery** and the **residence of the Catholic bishop** which has a collection of medieval artifacts worth a look (tel. 0285-22470).

The ⑥ ⑥ **Archaeological Museum** (◔ *8 am-2:30 pm, 500 drs. / € 1.47, tel. 0285-22725, closed Mon. & hols*)* should not be missed. It is housed in the old Jesuit school (Ecole des Frères) where the monks taught both Catholic and Orthodox boys between the 17th and 19th centuries. In the late 19th-early 20th c. it was converted in-

Panagia Myrtidiotissa

Archaeological Museum

Monastery-school of the Ursulines

Marco Sanudo's Palace

to a business school and it was here that the writer Nikos Kazantzakis studied briefly. The building was turned into a museum in 1973. Among its exhibits are ⑥ ⑥ **exceptional pottery** of the Mycenaean and Geometric periods, Archaic, Classical and Hellenistic ceramics, a fine collection of glass vessels from the Roman era, as well as a splendid collection of ⑥ ⑥ ⑥ **Early Cycladic marble idols**. The courtyard contains a **mosaic** from a 3rd c. AD Roman house, depicting a **Nereid riding a bull**. Also of interest are the ⑥ **Della Rocca-Barozzi Museum** in a Venetian mansion (open only in summer, tel. 0285-22387, Mr. Karavias) and the small **church of the Panagia Theoskepasti** with beautiful icons of the Cretan School, such as that of the Crucifixion (14th c.).

⑥ **Antico Veneziano** is an antiques shop in a basement dating from 1205, with Minoan columns and fragments from the ancient acropolis which predated the Kastro on the same site.

Crispi tower

Antico Veneziano

14

HISTORY OF THE KASTRO – MARCO SANUDO

The Kastro and the medieval town of Naxos were founded by Crusader Marco Sanudo and his knights when they assumed control of the Cyclades islands in 1207, after taking Constantinople. With the consent of the Frankish emperor, Sanudo became Duke of the Aegean Archipelago and thus the highest ranking Frankish lord in the region.

He built his fortress-city on the ruins of the ancient acropolis; initially it consisted of Sanudo's palace surrounded by the fortified dwellings of the nobles and other officers. It had the shape of a pentagon, with a tower in each of the five corners, while the houses on the perimeter formed its outer walls. The duke's vassals installed themselves outside and around the Kastro, while prosperous Orthodox families made up the nearby neighbourhoods Bourgo and Agora (whose old gates are still standing). The poor peasantry lived in Nio Horio (New Village) around Agia Kyriaki church. Later Jewish settlers built their homes in the Grotta and Fontana districts.

❷ EXCURSION: HALKI - APEIRANTHOS AND VICINITY

Halki-Akadimi-Kerami-Filoti-Zas Cave-Fotodoti monastery-Apeiranthos-Moutsouna (Psili Ammos)-Agia Kyriaki

⑥ ⑥ HALKI

Χαλκί / Halkí

The lovely historic village of **Halki**, 16 km east of Hora, was once the administrative centre of the district. Surrounded by an olive grove in a fertile inland valley, it has many buildings that played a role in the island's history, as well as windmills and **neoclassical mansions**. Here you will find the relatively well preserved ⑥ **Barozzi-Frangopoulos-Grazia tower-house** (16th-17th c.), whose first owners, descendants of the noble Venetian family Barozzi, exploited this fertile area, a fief of Filoti, to the hilt. The fortified dwelling has a tower and embrasures; its moat and drawbridge have long since vanished.

In the village centre you'll see the dazzling white church of the ⑥ ⑥ **Panagia Protothroni**, with its curious, characteristically Naxian stepped facade. Inside

Barozzi-Frangopoulos-Grazia tower-house

Halki

15

there are frescoes from the 9th, 10th, 12th and 13th century. The synthronon in the sanctuary has provoked much discussion among Byzantine scholars, since it dates to the 9th or 10th c., upsetting the theory that this feature is typical of the Early Christian period.

If you have time, try to visit the hundred year old **Valandra distillery**, which used to export its spirits as far away as the USA. The plant is still in operation, producing liqueurs in a variety of strengths from the citrus fruit *(kitro)* in the traditional manner. Near the distillery is a path that will take you through an olive grove to the delightful 9th c. church of ⊚ ⊚**Agios Georgios Diasoritis** (ca. 1 km). It contains marvellous frescoes but is apt to be locked. You can also get there by road and 200 m of level path from the other side of Halki.

AKADIMI

Ακάδημοι / Akádimi

The hamlet of Akadimi, just beyond Kerami, boasts the ⊚**Markopolitis-Papadakis tower-house** (17th-18th c.), which along with the tower in Kerami is the only one on the island not built by the Venetians. It belonged to Markakis Politis, who was revered by the Greeks for leading revolts against the Ottomans between 1770 and 1802.

KERAMI

Κεραμί / Keramí

In the neighbouring village of **Kerami**, the ⊚ ⊚ **17th c. tower** is now a private museum owned by a Mr. Kalavros. It contains a surprising wealth of **paintings**, **objects** and **heirlooms** from the 14th c. and later. The owner is in residence in summer and may be kind enough to let you in for a visit. On the outskirts of Kerami there is a fine ⊚ ⊚ **10th c. Byzantine church** dedicated to the Holy Apostles (Agii Apostoli).

⊚ FILOTI

Φιλότι / Filóti

Filoti lies 6 km from Apeiranthos and 20 km from Hora. One of the island's largest villages, it is built on the slopes of Mt. Zas and has a splendid view of an emerald green valley which bears no resemblance to the usual Cycladic landscape. You might want to pause here for a look at the **Laritzi (Delastik) tower**, which is still lived in, and take a break in one of the traditional cafes under the plane trees in the square off the main road.

ZAS CAVE

Σπήλαιο Ζα / Spíleo Za

On Mt. Zas (Zeus) about 1 km outside Filoti. After the crossroads, the road to the summit branches off to the cave (signposted) and then stops before the steep path that leads to it some 700 m further. Unfortunately the cave has not been prepared for the public and archaeologists are still at work inside. If you decide to go there, on no account attempt to enter on your own. A guide is absolutely essential, the ter-

rain is slippery and a powerful torch will be needed if you are to see anything at all. The interior of the cave has an area of 4,100 sq. m. It possesses one enormous chamber, 115 m long, and a smaller one once used by the locals as a hideout during pirate raids. Its most stunning section is to be found higher up, in its upper part, where there are magnificent stalagmites, while the depths of the cave have yielded prehistoric artifacts and traces of religious rites. The cave was dedicated to Zeus Milosios.

© © MONASTERY OF CHRISTOS FOTODOTIS

**Μονή Χριστού Φωτοδότη /
Μονή Christoú Fotodóti**
2 km from the village of Danakos, south of Apeiranthos, over a decent dirt road. If you should come to a wire fence with a gate, don't forget to close it behind you or the sheep and goats will get out. The keys to the monastery are usually kept above the door.
This beautiful abandoned little **fortified monastery** sits on a hill with a view to the sea and the lesser Cyclades in the distance, in an idyllic setting with springs and lush vegetation, perfect for walks and contemplation.
Impressive in its design, the monastery was rich and powerful in Byzantine times and under the Franks. Legend has it that there was once an ancient fortress here and that the monastery was built by some Byzantine princess or by the empress Irene.

© © © APEIRANTHOS

Απείρανθος / Apíranthos
27 km from Hora. No cars permitted in the old district.
This charming marble-paved market village is one of the most beautiful in the Cyclades. It was founded at the foot of Mt. Fanari in the 10th c. by Cretan refugees. Rich in folklore, it also has particularly interesting architecture. A walk up its **marble-flagged lanes** will go a long way towards revealing its magic, since you'll come to five museums; a ruined **Venetian castle** of the 13th c., known as Our Lady Aperatheitissa; **Venetian manor houses**, such as the © 17th c. **Zevgoli** (Kastri-Somarippa) **tower** and the © **Bardani** (Sforza-Kastri) tower, also 17th c., with the coat of arms of the Leontos family; two-storey stone houses with flower-filled courtyards and "twin" chimneys, gothic arches, attractive cafes, old churches and pretty

Our Lady Aperatheitissa

A marble-paved lane

The square with the plane trees

small piazzas, like the ⑥ ⑥ **square** with the plane trees. We suggest you end your stroll at Lefteri's wonderful restaurant, which doubles as a cafe-pastry shop.

Of the museums *(which are not always open as advertised between 8:30 and 2:30 owing to lack of staff)*, the most rewarding are the ⑥ ⑥ **Archaeological Museum**, with prehistoric finds, pottery and stone plaques with relief decoration, and the ⑥ **Geological Museum**, which has a big selection of minerals from Naxos, Greece and other parts of the world. But do take a quick look at the other three, the **Museum of Natural History**, the **Folklore Museum** and the **Museum of Handicrafts**, where you can buy beautiful embroideries.

The most distinctive churches in Apeiranthos are the ⑥ **Panagia Apeirathiotissa**, one of the island's oldest, with its fine icon screen and post-Byzantine icons, the **Panagia Katapoliani** and the **Panagia Theoskepasti** (both 17th c.).

⑥ MOUTSOUNA

Μουτσούνα / Moutsoúna

11 km from Apeiranthos, Moutsouna itself is a picturesque Cycladic village with rooms for tourists, little tavernas serving fresh fish, sandy and pebbly coves and extraordinary beaches nearby, most notably ♈ ♈ ♈ **Psili Ammos** *(see Best Beaches, p. 40)*.

The drive down to the coast is breathtaking, as the scenery changes constantly, while before you is a panoramic view of the Aegean with several islands in the distance. Alongside the road you'll notice the funicular used to transport emery from the quarries near Apeiranthos to the port where it was loaded onto ships. It ceased functioning in 1989.

AGIA KYRIAKI

Αγία Κυριακή / Αγία Kyriakí
Ask someone in Apeiranthos to show you the path to this beguiling little church (about 1 hour's walk). It has 9th c. frescoes depicting birds and fish, in compliance with the Iconoclasts' ban on the human figure. If you continue on another 15 minutes, you'll come to **Kalloni**, a beauty-spot with springs and plane trees.

❸ THE HEART OF NAXOS

The circular route we propose here is fairly long and includes most of the major landmarks and sights in the interior of Naxos. This is the island's most fertile area, with the villages and hamlets of central Naxos, a host of noteworthy Byzantine monuments and churches ranging from the 6th to the 11th century, as well as vestiges of its ancient heritage. We suggest that you make this tour with an experienced local taxi driver who is familiar with the sights, because many of these are located outside the villages and will be hard to find on your own. To see the principal landmarks you will need 3-4 hours. But to really get to know the area, two or more days will be necessary.

MELANES

Μέλανες / Mélanes
A lush village 8 km east of Hora, set in a fertile valley with olive groves, orchards, streams and old water mills.

ⓖ ⓖ KALAMITSIA

Καλαμίτσια / Kalamítsia
A partially signposted dirt road starting at the top of Melanes leads to **Kalamitsia**, 2 km away. Here, in a ravine with springs from which water runs even in summer, stands a half-ruined yet imposing 17th c. **palatial mansion** with thick stone walls and arches. It was the summer retreat of the Jesuit monks.

ⓖ KOUROUNOHORI

Κουρουνοχώρι / Kourounohóri
In this village, which is also close to Melanes, you'll see the **fortified residence** of the Mavroyenis family and the ⓖ **Marco Sanudo-Frangopoulos-Della Rocca "country" mansion**, which bears an inscription commemorating the visit in 1833 of King Otto. The Frankish **Karavias tower-house** lies behind the hill.
A beautiful path starts from **Kourounohori** to the Archaic ⓖ **Kouros of Melanes**, which if you have an hour to spare is the perfect approach to it.

THE KOUROS OF MELANES

**Κούρος των Μελάνων /
Koúros ton Melánon**
Not far from Melanes, at the hamlet of Myli, this ancient Greek youth lies "sleeping" next to a luxuriant veg-etable and flower garden. The statue, which is 6.5 m tall, was discovered when the owners of the property were tilling their soil in 1943. It was roughly hewn at the Flerios marble quarry nearby in the 7th or 6th c. BC, but for some rea-son was never finished or delivered to its intended destination. You can have a drink in the little **garden cafe** and then walk on to a second unfinished kouros a bit higher up.

KINIDAROS

Κινίδαρος / Kinídaros
Continuing on the road from Kourounohori, you'll come to Kinidaros, a well-wa-tered village smothered in greenery and known for its musicians and church fairs *(panigyria)*. To the north of the village, after an hour's walk *(see Walks and Hiking, p. 29)*, you'll find yourself in the verdant valley of Halandron, from which rises one of the island's largest and most impressive basilicas, **Agios Artemios** (18th c.). The chapel of **Agios Dimitrios** stands alongside it.

MARBLE QUARRIES

**Λατομεία Μαρμάρου /
Latomía Marmárou**
The ancient marble quarries are situated a short distance south of Kinidaros, at Flerios. This was the source of the marble from which the skilful Naxian sculptors chiselled so many of the astonishing statues, monuments and architectural or-naments we see today in museums and archaeological sites in many parts of Greece. The famous **Lions of Delos**, the **Treasury of the Naxians at Delphi**, the **massive kouroi** and the delicate **Early Cycladic idols** are just a few of the count-less masterpieces the island's much sought-after craftsmen bequeathed to humanity. The quarries at Emboli or Amboli near Apollonas were also important.

PANAGIA DROSIANI MONASTERY

Μονή Παναγιάς της Δροσιανής / Moní Panayiás Drosianís
In principle the church is open from 9 am-6 pm from early May to October 20. However, you may have to call 0285-32195 to get someone to unlock it. And be prepared to wait!
This unusual church lies 20 km from Hora, below the small hill village of **Moni**. It is

one of the oldest and most important Byzantine monuments in Europe. The original monastery was founded in the 6th-7th c.; what we see today is a 10th c. construction. Of the later buildings erected round it in the 12th c., nothing remains. From the outside the church seems a bewildering collection of domes and apses, a result of its eventual union with three adjoining chapels. Its rough-hewn stones give it an almost primitive appearance.

Inside, its dark walls are covered with rare ⑤ **frescoes**, some of which date back to the period before the Iconoclast Controversy and depict non-stylized human figures. Look for the one portraying the Virgin holding a disk bearing an icon of Christ. Painted at different times, sometimes on overlapping layers, the frescoes range in age from the 9th to 15th c.

⑤ ANO POTAMIA

Άνω Ποταμιά / Άno Potamiá

A detour off the main road after Halki will take you to this pretty village, which resembles a vast garden, a true paradise with springs and streams, attractive little houses, little churches and a sprinkling of fortified mansions. Next to it a river has carved out a ravine, whose banks are thick with leafy plane trees and other tall venerable trees.

Near Ano Potamia, a crumbling fortress — ⑤ **(A)pano Kastro** — occupies the site of an ancient acropolis, a point from which all of central Naxos can be seen. You can get there by following a path from **Tsikalario** *(see Castles and Tower-houses, p. 30)*.

⑤ ⑤ THE AREA SOUTH OF SANGRI

Just outside Sangri (if you're coming from Halki), you'll meet a junction beside a petrol station where you should turn left towards Agiassos. Almost immediately you'll see looming on your left the austere, almost windowless bulk of the ⑤ **Timios Stavros monastery** (16th c.). Although it is sometimes opened for exhibitions, you may have to ask its owners, the Bazaios family who live in one of the nearby houses, for the key. The family also own a collection of ecclesiastical memorabilia which they put on display on the day of the True Cross, September 14.

From there half an hour's walk will take you to the extremely old, abandoned ⑤ **monastery of the Panagia Kaloreitsa** or Kaloritissa (11th-13th c.), built in a stunning setting in a natural cavern on Prophitis Ilias hill. Not only is it interesting architecturally, it has rare post-Byzantine frescoes of the 17th c.

Near Timios Stavros, in a field on the right of the road toward the south, sits the long forgotten domed Byzantine ⑤ **chapel of Agios Artemios**, which is decorated with nonfigurative representations of spirals, volutes, leaves and rhomboids dating from the period of the Iconoclasts (8th-9th c.).

Archaic temple of Demeter

Two kilometres further, the road leads to the partially restored ⓖ ⓖ **Archaic temple of Demeter** (6th c. BC), which was used for ceremonial rites. Climbing the steps of a beautifully paved and landscaped path, you'll arrive at the temple where the restoration work is continuing. Some of the finds from the site and from Early Christian churches in the vicinity can be seen in the new museum to the left of the temple. Nearby, the Byzantine chapel of ⓖ **Agios Ioannis Theologos** was erected using marble from the temple.

The road from the temple of Demeter continues to the Gyroula district and will lead you to the south of Ano Sangri.

ⓖ ANO SANGRI

Άνω Σαγκρί / Áno Sangrí

Built on a wooded hill with a pleasant view, this village boasts windmills, picturesque houses and important Byzantine and Venetian monuments.

In the village itself is the old deserted ⓖ **monastery of Agios Eleftherios**, which was once a considerable religious and intellectual centre. Not far to the north of the village, over a rutted lane, stands the restored ⓖ **Palaiologos tower (17th c.)**. The owners are usually in residence in August and may allow you to see the ⓖ ⓖ **interior**, giving you a fascinating glimpse of another era.

ⓖ ⓖ ⓖ CHURCH OF AGIOS MAMAS (9th c.)

Εκκλησία Αγίου Μάμα / Ekklisía Ayíou Máma

Situated approximately midway between Sangri and Galanado. To get there you'll have to walk on the only path for about 45 minutes; the uphill return will take about an hour.

If you stop on the right side of the road underneath the sign, you'll be able to make out this pretty church in the valley below some 2 kilometres away. Of enormous interest architecturally, it is dedicated to Agios Mamas, the patron saint of shepherds.

This cross-in-square-type church is one of the oldest on the island and contains some noteworthy frescoes. It is said that it was the Orthodox cathedral until 1207, when the Franks converted it into a Catholic church. The building next to Agios Mamas was the country estate/residence of the Latin bishops of Naxos.

ⓖ BELONIA TOWER-HOUSE

Πύργος Μπελόνια / Pírgos Belónia

This imposing 17th c. fortified mansion commands the hillside above ⓖ **Galanado** and the fertile Livadia plain with a view of Hora and the sea. It belonged to the Venetian lord of the district and may be visited in summer with the owner's permission. Next to the mansion you'll see the charming little "twin" **church of Agios Ioannis**. One of its chapels is Orthodox, the other Catholic.

SANCTUARY OF IRIA

Ιερό των Ιρίων / Ieró ton Iríon

8 am -2:30 pm from May to September or in winter by arrangement with the Archaeological Museum (Mr. Koutelieris, tel. 0285-22725).

West of the road linking Galanado with the village of Glinado, off the road between Hora and the airport and next to the Naxos Holiday hotel, there is a decent dirt road that will take you to the ruins of the once important ancient shrine of Iria (ca. 1.5 km). The original structure was most probably built in the 7th c. BC and expanded a century later. Although it is not known to which deity the sanctuary was dedicated, some say it belonged to Dionysos. It remained in use through Roman times.

EXCURSION: HORA-APOLLONAS

This route follows the rugged coastline of northwest Naxos and will give you the chance to discover remote monasteries, romantic tower-houses and delightful coves *(see Best Beaches, p. 39-40).*

CHRYSOSTOMOS MONASTERY (17th c.)

Μονή Χρυσοστόμου / Moní Chrissostómou
This convent 3 km outside Hora is easily accessible from the road. A solid, fortified complex, it has a marvellous **view** of the sea and the Hora. It possesses a supposedly miraculous icon of St. Chrysostom. Near the convent is a chapel called **Theologaki**, a photographer's delight since it has been carved out of a cave on a rocky knoll. The road comes to within 200 metres of it.

YPSILIS MONASTERY OR ANGELAKOPOULOS TOWER (16th c.)

Μονή Υψηλής ή Πύργος Αγγελακόπουλου /
Moní Ipsilís or Pírgos Angelakópoulou
Getting to this fortified monastery is a bit tricky. Although a caretaker is usually present and the monastery itself is open and may be visited, access is via a private dirt road near the village of Engares through another property whose owner is not so welcoming. If you decide to ignore the No Trespassing signs and enter, look for an old low wooden gate with a metal lining near the greenhouses facing the beach of Amyti a bit higher up the mountainside. This is the way to the monastery but proceed at your own risk!

The monastery was built in 1660 by the Kokkos family. It has an exceptionally interesting interior and was initially dedicated to the Panagia Ypsilotera (Our Lady in the Highest). Because of its virtually impregnable design — it is the most heavily fortified building on the island — it was often used as a fortress-refuge where the Naxians sought refuge from pirates. And when the country people rose up against the Venetians, it was also here that they fled for protection.

The interior is divided into two levels around a court or **atrium**, which is approached by a dark, narrow corridor beginning at the entrance. The other three sides are occupied by cells and storerooms. Rising out of the southwest corner is a cylindrical tower with bat-

tlements, embrasures and a platform from where boiling oil could be poured on would-be assailants. The tower communicates with the flat roof via a low door and with the atrium by an internal stone staircase. Mid way down the fourth side of the atrium stands the monastery church, a **post-Byzantine chapel**. This evocative setting is completed by stone windowsills, ledges and **half-moon ogival arches**.

PANAGIA FANEROMENI MONASTERY (17th c.)

**Μονή Παναγίας Φανερωμένης /
Moní Panayías Faneroménis**

☺ *every day throughout the year 10 am -12 noon and 5-7:30 pm, in August 8 am - 1 pm and 5 - 9 pm, tel. (0285) 63266.*
You can get here from Ypsilis Monastery by taking the paved road a few kilometres further. Beautiful, dazzling white and in good condition, with stunning interiors, rare icons and a library.

AGIAS TOWER AND MONASTERY

**Πύργος Αγιάς - Μονή Αγιάς /
Pirgos Ayiás - Moni Ayiás**
The Agias fortified mansion dominates a strategic point between cape Abrami and Apollonas, controlling the northernmost section of the island. It lies alongside the road on your left; you can't miss it. Down a short, thickly shaded path from the tower is the tiny **church of Agias** dedicated to the Virgin, next to a bubbling spring. The low buildings nearby were once monks' cells. The tower is picturesque but abandoned.

APOLLONAS

Απόλλωνας / Apóllonas
34 km from Hora, on the coast road. Apollonas is a small resort built above a beach on the cove of the same name *(see Best Beaches, p. 40)*. Trees shade some of the small simple hotels and rented rooms, while there is also a little mole for boats. The area was known in antiquity for its good

quality marble, hewn from the **quarries** near Emboli or Amboli hill. Many of the most talented sculptors of the day created the marvellous works dedicated to Delos at this spot. A bit to the north of the hill you can still make out the battered remains of a medieval castle called Kalogeros or the Monk.

⑥ ⑥ THE KOUROS OF APOLLONAS

**Κούρος του Απόλλωνα /
Κούros tou Apóllona**
To see this enormous (11 m) unfinished statue of a
young man, follow the signs (or the other sightseers)
up a slope on the outskirts of the village. Here
stretched out in a hollow surrounded by rocks is the
⑥ ⑥ **Archaic Kouros** (7th-6th c. BC), which is
thought to be older than the Melanes Kouros. Why it
never left the site remains an enigma.

⑥ EMERY MINES

Σμυριδωρυχεία / Smirithorihía
*If you wish to continue as far as Ko-
ronos, you can take a look at the emery
quarries between Koronos and Lionas. If
time is a factor, the return to Hora is
shorter and quicker over the coast road.
Also, bear in mind that the public bus
from Apeiranthos to Moutsouna stops
at the entrance to the mines.*

Just before you arrive at the mines, on
your left below the road you'll see the
unloading station and warehouses
where the emery was delivered. It's also
a favourite spot with the tour buses
which stop here to let their passengers
feel the weight of the stones with their
own hands. Emery is an especially hard
mineral, second only to diamonds in
strength.

The mining of emery was once a source of wealth for the island and many locals
worked in the quarries. From here the stones embarked on their aerial journey down
to the harbour at Moutsouna and from there to points round the world. Emery used to
have many applications in industry (and was particularly used for polishing — re-
member the emery board?); today however artificial materials have taken its place.
The funicular line with its buckets is still standing. When it stopped operating in
1989, large quantities of emery were left abandoned in the warehouses.

❺ THE SUMMER RESORTS OF SOUTHWEST NAXOS

An immense, almost unbroken beach extends from Hora for more than 25 kilometres
until it finally ends at Agiassos. Most of this coastline consists of delightful sandy
coves, big and small.
You'll find information and descriptions of the resorts and their beaches, which draw
the lion's share of visitors to Naxos during the summer, in the chapter on *Best-
Beaches, pp. 37-39.*

OTHER THINGS
TO DO

SPARE TIME

Cinema: Good films are often shown at the Cine Astra open-air cinema in Hora.
Music: Father Manolis Remoundos organizes concerts of classical and other types of music in the Kastro. For information call (0285) 22470.
Photography classes: Britisher Stuart Thorpe leads expeditions to particularly photogenic locations and gives on-the-spot practical lessons in English and in German. For information, call the Orkos Hotel (0285) 75321.
Visit to the Della Rocca pharmacy: This fascinating old apothecary shop is on the Hora waterfront.

SPORTS

The southwest coast — from Agios Georgios, Agios Prokopis and Agia Anna as far as Mikri Vigla — is a windsurfer's dream come true. Equipment can be rented at Agios Prokopis and Agia Anna.

WALKS AND HIKING

Here we outline just a few of the island's walks. If you're interested in finding out more, we suggest you get in touch with an experienced guide who knows the paths well, such as Ms. Elisabeth Stanley (0285) 22481.

Information and detailed descriptions of many interesting routes can be found in Christian Ucke's excellent book, Walking Tours on Naxos.

⑥ ⑥ ⑥ **Temple of Artemis-Engares:** Start out from the ancient temple below the village of Kinidaros. Take a look at the large but ruined ⑥ ⑥ **basilica of Agios Artemios** (and the adjoining chapel of Agios Dimitrios) and then follow the red markings below the little bridge next to the stream and walk until you come to **Langada**, a pretty spot with a spring, turtles and ducks. A bit further on you'll see an abandoned village with a watermill, surrounded by greenery and plane trees before reaching the village of Engares. The walk takes about 2 hours and is relatively difficult. You can of course also do it the other way.

Engares

☺ ☺ ☺ **Koronis (Komniaki)-Abrami cove:** A walk with views of the island's north coast. You'll breathe herb-scented mountain air, you'll walk along a marble-paved pathway with steps, and you'll see lots of wild flowers, greenery and big (harmless) lizards. Estimated time needed, about 3 hours.

☺ ☺ **Koronis (Komniaki)-Apollonas:** This path cuts across 7 km of hillside through verdant scenery with plenty of trees. Estimated time needed, about 2 1/2 hours.

☺ ☺ **Kourounohori-Myli:** A good footpath taking you past orchards, wild flowers and even five mini-waterfalls as far as Myli and the **Kouros**. An easy walk taking only 1 hour.

☺ ☺ **Apeiranthos-Panagia Fanariotissa:** This chapel high on Mt. Fanari has a stupendous view of the Aegean from an altitude of 900 m. Estimated time needed, about 2 1/2 hours.

☺ ☺ **Melanes-Kalamitsia:** From Melanes you reach this once mighty fortified complex (1650), the former summer retreat of the Jesuits. Estimated time needed, 45 minutes. You can also get here by car.

☺ **Ano Potamia-Kato Potamia:** Follow the road next to the river, a pleasant stroll amongst trees with ducks for company. Estimated time needed, 1 hour.

☺ **Stavros Keramotis-Mavro Vouni:** Start out from the church at the crossroads on the main road above Keramoti. The path goes up to the summit of Mavro Vouni (Black Mountain). If you continue on, you can reach Komniani (Koronis). The whole walk should take about 5-6 hours.

☺ **Apeiranthos-Fotodotis monastery:** A path with a spectacular view takes you to the fortified monastery of Ai Yiannis Fotodotis (estimated time needed, 1 1/2 hours).

CASTLES AND TOWER–HOUSES

☺ ☺ **Apalyros Castle:** Accessible only by a steep, difficult path (estimated time needed, about 2 hours), this Byzantine castle lies off the dirt road between Filoti and Kalados bay at the southern tip of the island. It perches like an eagle's nest on the top of a wind-battered rock — the site of an ancient acropolis, which explains the presence of the large amounts of marble used in its construction. From this strategic position it was possible to control almost all the south end of Naxos. Its thick circuit walls are still standing, along with some ruined buildings, turrets, a Byzantine church and cisterns. When in 1207 Marco Sanudo and his Venetian fortune-seeking cohorts landed on the island, the castle was in the hands of Genoese pirates, who defended it so vigorously that the ensuing siege lasted about five weeks. To bring it to a close, Marco Sanudo burned his ships, leaving his warriors no alternative but to capture the castle and the whole island.

⑥ ⑥ **Apano Kastro (Upper Castle):** Another difficult ascent, this one's shorter by 1 hour. This is the most interesting fortress on the island, having been in service in ancient and Byzantine times as well as Venetian; unfortunately it is now in ruins. Under the Venetians and later, it was a small medieval town with walls and three concentric defence walls, turrets, embrasures, fountains, arches, cisterns for water, wine and olive oil, and four Byzantine churches, some bearing traces of old frescoes. There are also vestiges of Cyclopean walls, ancient cemeteries and tombs from the Mycenaean and Geometric periods.

On the eastern slopes, at Alonakia, you will see an upright rock or megalithic monument (menhir). Menhirs were erected in prehistoric times and there are many theories concerning their function. Some scholars believe they were used as shrines or stelae honouring certain deities, others think they were tombstones commemorating the death of mortals. Still others maintain that they were aids in plotting celestial movements or boundary markers.

⑥ **Heimarros Tower:** You'll spot the fort on the left side of the dirt road between Filoti and Kalados. This four-storeyed marble fortress dates from Hellenistic times and was erected by Ptolemy, the Macedonian ruler of Egypt. It is still in fairly good condition despite its wild, deserted setting, south of Mt. Zas. If you wish to inspect it more closely, you'll need about 3 hours to walk there from Filoti.

CHURCHES AND MONASTERIES

⑥ ⑥ **Panagia Daminiotissa (11th-12th c.):** 15 km east of Hora, near Halki. This charming little church boasts both interesting architecture and fine frescoes. It is situated in the Daminos estate, on the outskirts of Kaloxylo village.

⑥ **Prophitis Ilias, formerly Panagia Vlaherniotissa (12th-13th c.):** In Hora, near the waterfront, behind the Commercial (Emboriki) Bank. The church contains a beautiful wooden icon screen and wonderful icons painted by Angelos, a pupil of El Greco. Note the coat of arms of the Palaiologos dynasty with its cross and 4 Bs above the entrance.

⑥ **Agios Antonios o Eremitis (13th c.):** A Catholic church in Hora, near the harbour. It was built by the Knights of St. John of Rhodes.

⑥ **Agios Thalelaios (13th c.):** Located about 5 km east of Hora on the road to Angida and Kourounohori.

⑥ **Agios Ioannis o Theologos (13th c.):** You'll find this church in the village of Kerami, which lies between Halki and Filoti. A simple domed chapel, it contains lovely frescoes.

⑥ **Panagia Arkouliotissa or Arkoulou (14th c.):** This small but extraordinary chapel lies outside Sangri, on the road to Agiassos.

Agios Antonios o Eremitis

Οther Τhings to Do

EXCURSIONS TO NEARBY ISLANDS

Think about taking a trip to the Minor Cyclades Islands — Donousa, Koufonissia, Schinousa and Iraklia — or Amorgos — which are all quite close to Naxos. Paros, Syros, Santorini, Mykonos and Delos are also within easy reach. *For information, see How to Get There, Connections, p. 58.*

MINOR EASTERN CYCLADES

Pirate lairs in earlier centuries, abandoned outposts in the more recent past, these islands are fast becoming the latest "in" places thanks to their superb beaches and unspoiled landscapes. If you avoid travelling between 15 July and 20 August, you're sure to enjoy the "small is beautiful" experience. The islands are linked with Amorgos, Mykonos, Paros and Piraeus in addition to Naxos.

⊚ ⊚ DONOUSA

Δονούσα / Donoúsa
Donousa has only 120 inhabitants but lots to offer. Its sights include the **church of the Panagia** with its stunning view, the **Tihos Cave**, the **Spring** and the **Seal Cave** (Fokospilia). The swimming is excellent at **Vlyhos**, **Mesa Ammos** and **Sapounochroma** (near the hamlet of Kalotaritisssa), and Livadi beach near the village of Mersini.

⊚ ⊚ PANO KOUFONISSI

The town beach

Πάνω Κουφονήσι/ Páno Koufoníssi
Having the best beaches in the group, not surprisingly it also attracts the biggest crowds. The little island, once a notorious pirate hideout, today has a permanent population of 250 people. It is considered the most picturesque and most fashionable of these islands. Here you'll find little bars, tavernas and great beaches, starting with the village ♀♀**beach**, ♀♀**Harokopos** and ♀♀**Italida**, but also the more distant, quieter beaches of ♀♀♀**Pori** and ♀♀**Fanos**.

⊚ KATO KOUFONISSI

Κάτω Κουφονήσι / Káto Koufoníssi
This tiny island is deserted in winter, in summer only a few fishermen call it home. It is worth taking a caique to lovely ♀♀**Nero** beach and dining at its wonderful **little taverna**. We can guarantee a memorable evening with good food and drink at the water's edge. The caique leaves around midnight for Pano Koufonissi.

⑥ SCHINOUSA

Σχοινούσα / Skinousa
This islet has three tiny villages, pretty churches like the **Panagia Akathi**, and very good, tranquil beaches, such as ♓ ♓ ♓ **Psili Ammos** (which you can walk to), ♓ ♓ **Almyros** and **Fontana** on the east coast, as well as ♓ **Tsingouri**, **Livadi** and **Aligaria** on the southwest.

⑥ IRAKLIA

Ηρακλειά / Irakliá
A small island with two villages and about 100 inhabitants, Iraklia has lovely beaches and two fascinating caves. One of them, the so-called **Cave of Polyphemus the Cyclops** (or **Ai-Yiannis**) is among the most magnificent in the Aegean (2,000 sq. m) with stalactites, sta-

Iraklia

lagmites and a little lake. You can also take a walk to the castle and then have a dip at pretty ♓ ♓ **Livadi beach** down below. Other good beaches include **Spilia**, **Vourkaria**, **Alimia** and **Meriha**, beside a high sheer cliff.

If you have a boat, you can also explore the rest of the islands in the area, all of which are uninhabited — Antikeros, Dryma, Tris Makaries and Daskalio. Of greatest interest is ⑥ **Keros**, which was once a major Early Cycladic kingdom. Because of its importance to archaeologists it is forbidden to camp or picnic there, and naturally no building has taken place.

ORGANIZED TOURS

NAXOS TOURS

Hora, tel. (0285) 23043, 23743, 22095, fax 23951
One-day cruises to Delos and Mykonos, Santorini, Amorgos and the Koufonissia. Also on offer are round-the-island excursions by boat and one-day Robinson Crusoe camping expeditions. Departures from Naxos port in the morning, returning in the afternoon.

ZAS TRAVEL

Hora, tel. (0285) 23330-1
Here you can join a day-long bus trip around Naxos with a guide to the most important sights, as well as one-day cruises to Delos and Mykonos and Santorini. Departures from the port in the morning, returning in the afternoon.

CHURCH FESTIVALS AND OTHER EVENTS

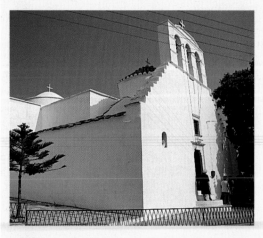

February-March

Carnival: Celebrated in Apeiranthos and Filoti with Dionysiac echoes, partying and dancing. Some men drape themselves with sheepbells, filling the streets with a frightful clangour; others are dressed as old women, bear tamers and bears, with bells round their necks, while still others tease onlookers with improvised satirical jibes and jokes. Clean Monday, the start of Lent, is a day of dancing, singing and parties all over the island, with dances led by men decked out in ribbons and gilt coins.

June
- **23 June**, at Apeiranthos: May wreaths fuel the bonfires of St. John.
- **29 June**, at Melanes: the big panigyri (festival) of the Holy Apostles, which lasts for three days.

July
- **7 July**, at Potamia: Panigyri in honour of St. Kyriaki.
- **8 July**, at Agios Prokopis: Panigyri in honour of St. Prokopios, with music and dancing.
- **14 July**, in Hora: Panigyri in honour of St. Nikodimos, one of the biggest on the island, with dancing and live music performed by local groups.
- **15 July-5 August**, in Hora: The Dionysia cultural festival with exhibitions, theatre, concerts and sports events.
- **25 July**, at Agia Anna: Panigyri in honour of St. Anne, with music and dancing.
- **26 July**, at Kinidaros: Panigyri in honour of St. Paraskevi, with music and dancing.

August
- **6 August**, at Kourounohori: Panigyri commemorating the Transfiguration of the Saviour.
- **15 August**, at Filoti, Apeiranthos and Agia monastery: Panigyria in honour of the Virgin. The celebrations at Filoti last 3 days and are among the island's most festive.
- **29 August**, at Apeiranthos: Panigyri in honour of St. John.

September
- **8 September**, at Moni: Panigyri in honour of the Panagia Drosiani.
- **14 September**, at Galanado: Panigyri in honour of the True Cross.

BEST BEACHES

Some of Greece's most superlative beaches are to be found in Naxos, something few Greeks are aware of, but which many foreigners have already discovered. Most of them lie near Hora and on the south coast, which has the largest concentration of hotels, restaurants and rooms. However, there are also exceptional beaches on the southeastern coast, which has remained practically untouched by tourism. Finally, the north coast boasts a number of attractive little coves.

SOUTH OF HORA

In geographical order

☂ AGIOS GEORGIOS

Άγιος Γεώργιος / Άyios Yórgios
This is the Hora beach. About 1 kilometre long, it is a fully equipped stretch of sand which is usually swarming with sunbathers. It is also the island's **windsurfing centre** with cafe-bars where surfers hang out and compare notes.

☂ ☂ ☂ AGIOS PROKOPIS

Άγιος Προκόπης / Άyios Prokópis
About 7 km from Hora, this is a large, organized and very beautiful beach with marvellous coarse sand in the water and out, which neither sticks to your body or blows in your eyes when it's windy. Once it was one of Greece's most superb beaches and it could still be if it were not so popular. Happily, the crowds thin out about midway down the beach and at the other end past the (usually waterless) lagoon. The beach ends at the holiday resort where there are umbrellas, tavernas and accommodation.

☂ ☂ AGIA ANNA

Αγία Άννα / Αγία Άnna
8 km from Hora. Another large, beautiful, organized sandy beach, which is more or less a continuation of Agios Prokopis. Like it, some sections of Agia Anna are very crowded. The seemingly endless sand is interrupted only by the picturesque fishing port-resort where there are several tavernas. In summer access and parking can be problematic because the road is so narrow. You can also get there by boat from Hora.

Rock Formations south of Mikri Vigla

🌂🌂🌂 PLAKA

Πλάκα / Pláka

Enormous (4 km!), lovely, quiet, Plaka begins where Agia Anna ends, and is only organized at a few spots where there are hotels, umbrellas and tavernas. Its golden sands extend the length of a narrow dirt road that tunnels through the high reeds that block out the sea. This was once the favourite of campers, hippies and nudists. Today there are only a few of the latter, who keep to the more isolated areas.

🌂🌂🌂 MIKRI VIGLA 🌂🌂 ORKOS

Μικρή Βίγλα / Mikrí Vígla - Ορκός / Orkós

16 km from Hora. The prettiest resort in southwest Naxos, with tavernas, rooms and two large sandy beaches with translucent water, one on either side of the little rocky cape. The northern one, **Parthenos** (or Virgin), is often buffeted by the north winds *(meltemia)* and is thus heaven for windsurfers. The southern and equally attractive **Mikri Vigla** (or **Limanaki**) beach is protected from the wind and organized. Together the beaches stretch for 4 kilometres.

The sculpted rocks on the cape and the charming 🌂🌂 **sandy mini coves** around the little resort of **Orkos**, between Plaka and Mikri Vigla, add extra variety to your choice of bathing spots.

🌂🌂 KASTRAKI (GLYFADA)

Καστράκι (Γλυφάδα) / Kastráki (Glifáda)

17 km from Hora. This brand-new resort is of no particular interest, but its three kilometres of beach are wonderful. Its fine sand stretches from Kastraki as far as Alyko with umbrellas available at certain points and some tavernas a bit higher up. Some 300 m away the **Oskelos tower** and the remains of a **Cyclopean-walled Mycenaean acropolis** can be seen atop a hill with a fine view. One of the surprising sights in the vicinity is a **farm where ostriches are raised**.

🌂🌂 ALYKO

Αλυκό / Alíkó

The natural continuation of Kastraki beach, Alyko has an exotic south-sea atmosphere with its sand dunes and cedar woods. The impression is somewhat marred by the presence of the unfinished buildings of an abandoned hotel complex.

As you face the sea, to the left of the buildings is the only organized beach of the six in the vicinity. It is the largest and has fine white sand. To its right and to the right of the buildings you'll find the other five pretty beaches, all tucked into ☂ ☂ ☂ **delightful coves**, where you may surprise a few nudists.

☂ ☂ ☂ PYRGAKI

Πυργάκι / Pirgáki
21 km from Hora, a bit beyond Alyko, there are two fantastic sandy beaches bordering clean clear water and with few bathers, next to sand dunes and a marvellous cedar forest. The better of the two is the furthest away. It has been equipped with umbrellas et al by the Pyrgaki hotel on the hill above. At some distance from the sea but parallel to the beach is the budding **Pyrgaki resort**, which is as yet sparsely built with a few rooms and tavernas.

☂ AGIASSOS

Αγιασσός / Ayiassós
About 2 km from Kastraki. Another large quiet sandy beach with clear shallow water bordering a small dispersed resort. At the end of the road and beach you'll find the wonderful **Vrahia taverna**. The friendly proprietors, apart from serving good home cooking and fresh fish, also have some choice rooms available for rent.

NORTH OF HORA

On the lacy shore below the road between Hora and Apollonas you'll catch sight of **delightful little coves** enclosing sandy or pebbly beaches.
The only ones accessible by car are ☂ **Amyti beach** and ☂ **Abram(i) bay**, with its taverna and rooms, beloved by those who like out-of-the-way places, but somewhat exposed to the north winds.

Abrami bay

39

EASTERN NAXOS

Apart from Apollonas, eastern Naxos is little visited by tourists.

⛱ APOLLONAS

Απόλλωνας / Apóllonas
About 50 km from Hora. A small, rather crowded beach with tavernas at the water's edge and some rooms for rent.

⛱ MOUTSOUNA

Μουτσούνα / Moutsoúna
About 38 km from Hora and 11 km from Apeiranthos. Next to the cove around which the pretty little port is built, with its rooms and fish tavernas, there is a series of ⛱ ⛱ **lovely small beaches**. When the meltemi is not blowing, the neighbouring pebbly ⛱ **Azalas beach** is a good alternative, especially if you walk or drive down the dirt road to it. On its northern tip the pebbles give way to a perfect little ⛱ ⛱ **sandy stretch**.

⛱ ⛱ ⛱ PSILI AMMOS

Ψιλή Άμμος / Psilí Ámmos
From Moutsouna a dirt road takes you to the little hamlet of Psili Ammos. One kilometre past it, turn left towards the sand dunes. This spectacular beach is set in magic surroundings, next to a cedar wood and far from any annoying crowds or buildings.

⛱ ⛱ PANORMOS

Πάνορμος / Pánormos
The road is rutted and bumpy but, if your car can cope, you'll be rewarded by a beautiful little deserted beach at the end of it.

OTHER BEACHES

⛱ **Kalados bay**, in southern Naxos. Sailboats are usually at anchor offshore here and at ⛱ **Rina**, a sandy bay with palm trees, where fresh water flows down from the mountains. ⛱ **Kleidos** lies between Psili Ammos and Panormos, ⛱ **Pahia Ammos** is between Amyti beach and Abrami bay, on the north coast, and the little beach of ⛱ **Liona** next to the hamlet of that name in between Apollonas and Moutsouna.

Psili Ammos

BEST HOTELS
AND ROOMS

BEST LOCATION

Life on Naxos revolves round Hora and the nearby beach of Agios Georgios, where most of the hotels are to be found. Outside of Hora, the hotels are open only in summer so that if you visit Naxos at any other time of year, you will have no choice but to stay there. If you're seeking something quiet and near the sea, and are not particularly interested in nightlife, then you should be happy with a hotel in one of the summer resorts on the southwest coast, where there are so many excellent beaches to choose from. For even more tranquillity and less expensive accommodation, near exotic beaches, we recommend the Moutsouna area. Unfortunately, the villages in the interior do not yet offer rooms of a decent standard.

If you have trouble finding a room despite our extensive list, contact the Association of Naxos Hotelowners, tel. (0285) 25938, or the Association of Room Rentals, tel. (0285) 25985.

PRICES

The hotel prices mentioned below are the official ones, set by the National Tourist Organization for a double room, in the low and high season, without breakfast. Since owners are allowed to modify prices, always try to negotiate with them.

HORA - AGIOS GEORGIOS

✓✓✓ PORTO NAXOS (A Class)

Tel. (0285) 23970-2, fax 23973
Open: All year long. **Description:** The best hotel in Naxos, modelled along the lines of a Cycladic village. Situated outside Hora, some distance from the sea on the road to the airport. **Rooms:** 33 rooms, with A/C, TV, mini bar and telephone. **Special features:** Restaurant, bar, pool, washing machine, safe box, tennis court, gym, foreign exchange, lounge and parking. **Price:** 38,000-58,000 drs. (€ 111.52-170.21). **Value for money:** ✱ ✱ **Credit cards:** All.

✔✔ HOTEL NISSAKI BEACH (C Class)

Agios Georgios beach
Tel. (0285) 25710-4
Fax 23876

Open: April-October. **Description:** Simple, decent hotel, the biggest at Agios Georgios. Built in Cycladic style near the sea, at the beginning of the beach. The owner is president of the Hotelowners Association. **Rooms:** 38 rooms, with A/C, TV and telephone. **Special features:** Good restaurant and service, bar, pool, washing machine, foreign exchange, free transport to and from Hora. **Price:** 17,000-23,000 drs. (€ 49.89-67.50). **Value for money:** ✱ ✱ **Credit cards:** Visa, Mastercard.

✔ HOTEL GROTTA (C Class)

In the Grotta district
Tel. (0285) 22215, 22201,
22101, fax 22000

Open: April-October. **Description:** Built on the low hill at Grotta in a wonderful location with views of the sea, Hora, the Kastro and the Portara. Good service by the owner's family. **Rooms:** 40 simple rooms, with fridge and balcony or veranda with a view. **Special features:** Free bus service to and from Hora, bar, room service, safe box, foreign exchange, TV in the lounge, and parking. **Price:** 12,000-18,000 drs. (€ 35.22-52.82). **Value for money:** ✱ ✱ **Credit cards:** Visa, Mastercard.

✔ HOTEL ASTERIA (C Class)

Agios Georgios beach, tel.
(0285) 23002, fax 22334

Open: April-October. **Description:** Simple but good seaside hotel complex in Cycladic style in a superb location above the beach. **Rooms:** 38 rooms, with TV, mini bar/fridge and telephone. **Special features:** Bar, lounge with TV, and free transport to and from Hora. **Price:** 15,000-23,000 drs. (€ 44.02-67.50). **Value for money:** ✱ ✱ ✱ **Credit cards:** Visa, Mastercard.

✓ HOTEL ALKYONI (B Class)

Agios Georgios beach
Tel. (0285) 26136, fax 25387, (01) 7790165, fax (0285) 23499
Open: May-October. **Description:** A new building with very attractive outdoor areas and one of Naxos's prettiest gardens. **Rooms:** 40 comfortable rooms, with A/C, telephone and fridge. Half the rooms have a splendid seaview. **Special features:** Taverna, bar, pool and kiddie pool, safe box and parking. **Price:** 15,000-27,500 drs. (€ 44.02-80.70), with breakfast. **Value for money:** ✸ **Credit cards:** None.

OTHER BEST SELECTIONS

✓ **APOLLON** *Tel. (0285) 25201.* In Hora, behind the waterfront near the Cathedral. Renovated in 2000. Good location with parking facilities. **Price:** 26,000-30,000 drs. (€ 76.30-88.04).

Chateau Zevgoli

✓ **CHATEAU ZEVGOLI** *Tel. (0285) 22993, 25201, 26123, fax 25200.* Small (10 rooms), charming hotel tucked into a Kastro alleyway, with tasteful furnishings and traditional decor. Equipped with a pretty courtyard, TV, telephone, bar, dry cleaners. **Price:** 22,000-28,000 drs. (€ 64.56-82.17), with breakfast.

✓ **HOTEL GALAXY** *Tel. (0285) 22422-4, fax 22889.* Cycladic architecture, renovated in 2000, just 50 m from Agios Georgios beach, 54 rooms with A/C, telephone, TV, bar, playground, pool and parking. **Price:** 21,000-36,000 drs. (€ 61.63-105.65)

✓ **STUDIOS SPIROS** *Tel. (0285) 24854, 25003, 26141.* At Koti, 200 m behind Agios Georgios beach. The studios are large with attractive decor; pool. **Price:** 10,000-15,000 drs. (€ 29.35-44.02)

Naxos Beach I

✓ **NAXOS HOLIDAYS** *Tel. (0285) 25790-1.* A sizeable hotel with 75 air conditioned rooms and a large pool. **Price:** 18,000-45,000 drs. (€ 52.82-132.06)

✓ **NAXOS BEACH I** *Tel. (0285) 22928, 24805.* Hotel-bungalow complex, 50 m from Agios Georgios beach. Renovated in 2000. **Price:** Upon request.

ALTERNATIVES

AEOLIS *Tel. (0285) 22321, 23601-3, fax 23600*. At Agios Georgios, not far from the beach. **Price: 19,000-32,000 drs. (€ 55.76-93.91)**

SUNIBEACH *Tel. (0285) 24350, 25790-1*. Near Agios Georgios, owned by Naxos Holidays. **Price: 14,000-25,000 drs. (€ 41.09-73.37)**, with breakfast.

HOTEL GLAROS *Tel. (0285) 23101, fax 24877*. Simple, well-run hotel complex, 25 m from Agios Georgios beach. Popular with the French. Fully equipped rooms with TV and telephone. **Price: 12,000-24,000 drs. (€ 35.22-70.43)**

MATHIASSOS VILLAGE *Tel. (0285) 22200, 23300, fax 24700*. Simple tourist hotel with a garden and bungalows in a good location on the main road out of Hora. With pool, bar, restaurant, tennis court, bus to and from the port, playground, lounge and parking. **Price: 11,200-22,200 drs. (€ 32.87-65.15)**

COLOSSEO *Tel. (0285) 24182, (0932) 637732* (Georgos). Simple studios in a good location near Agios Georgios beach. **Price: 10,000-22,000 drs. (€ 29.35-64.56)**

HOTEL ILIOVASILEMA *Tel. (0285) 23222-3, fax 23224*. At Agios Georgios, 100 m from the beach. **Price: 10,000-22,000 drs. (€ 29.35-64.56)**

HOTEL CORONIS *Tel. (0285) 22297*. Near OTE (Telephone Co bldg), on the Hora waterfront. **Price: 14,000-21,000 drs. (€ 41.09-61.63)**

AKROYIALI *Tel. (0285) 22321, 23601-3, fax 23600*. Well-run, 30 m from Agios Georgios beach, ideal for the price. **Price: 12,000-20,000 drs. (€ 35.22-58.69)**

ONEIRO *Tel. (0285) 24934*. Near the police station in Hora. Pleasant, neat and clean, inexpensive especially in June and September. **Price: 11,000-20,000 drs. (€ 32.28-58.69)**

GALINI *Tel. (0285) 22114, 22516, fax 22677*. On Agios Georgios beach. Good location, good price. **Price: 8,000-19,000 drs. (€ 23.48-55.76)**

ARGO *Tel. (0285) 25330-1, 23059, fax 24910*. At Agios Georgios, close to the beach. **Price: 9,000-18,000 drs. (€ 26.41-52.82)**

SOULA *Tel. (0285) 23196, fax 25786*. At Agios Georgios. **Price: 7,000-17,000 drs. (€ 20.54-49.89)**

PANORAMA *Tel. (0285) 22404, 22330, fax 24404*. In the Kastro (Hora), with a view of the port. Small, clean rooms, with A/C, some with veranda and view. **Price: 13,000-16,000 drs. (€ 38.15-46.96)**

ANIXIS *Tel. (0285) 22932*. In the heart of the Old Town. Simple, small, modern and clean, with a garden, balconies and views. Breakfast on the veranda. **Price: 11,000-15,000 drs. (€ 32.28-44.02)**

ANIXIS RESORT *Tel. (0285) 22112*. At Agios Georgios, not far from the beach. Under the same management as Anixis in Hora. **Price: 10,000-15,000 drs. (€ 29.35-44.02)**

CAMPING
NAXOS CAMPING *Tel. (0285) 23500-1*. At Agios Georgios, 200 m from the sea. Capacity: 100 pitches, 300 people. **Price: Upon request.**

APEIRANTHOS AND VICINITY

MOUTSOUNA

✓ OSTRIA STUDIOS

Tel. (0285) 68235, 61229, fax 68235
Open: May-October. **Description:** Situated on the outskirts of the village, near Moutsouna beach. Cycladic architecture, attractively furnished and laid out. Peaceful, ideal for families. **Rooms:** 12 fully-equipped rooms, with telephone, kitchenette and fridge, with a seaview. **Special features:** Garden and playground, taverna and parking area. **Price:** Upon request. **Value for money:** ❀ ❀ ❀ **Credit cards:** None.

ANOTHER BEST SELECTION

✓ AGERINO STUDIOS *Tel. (0285) 68255.* On Moutsouna beach, with a seaview and a taverna on the water's edge. **Price:** Upon request.

SOUTHWEST BEACHES

AGIOS PROKOPIOS

✓✓✓ NAXOS BEACH II (A Class)

At Stelida, 800 m from Agios Prokopis beach, tel. (0285) 26590, fax 24197
Open: April-October. **Description:** One of the island's best, with a splendid view of Hora. **Rooms:** 45 suites, with A/C, satellite TV, telephone, radio, fridge, kitchenette, hair dryer and safebox. **Special features:** Restaurant, bar, TV lounge, pool and pool bar, mini market, tennis court, parking. **Price:** Upon request. **Value for money:** ❀ **Credit cards:** All.

✓ HOTEL LIANOS VILLAGE (C Class)

At Stelida, 600 m from Agios Prokopis beach, tel. (0285) 23366, 23865, 26380, (0944) 501059, fax (0285) 26362
Open: May-October. **Description:** Large hotel complex modelled on a traditional Aegean village. Located on a hill above the beach with a gorgeous view. **Rooms:** 42 rooms with A/C, telephone, TV, mini bar, safebox and seaview. **Special fea-**

tures: Garden, bar, room service, pool and parking. **Price:** 15,000-36,000 drs. (€ 44.02-105.65). **Value for money:** ✿ ✿ **Credit cards:** Visa, Mastercard.

OTHER BEST SELECTIONS

✓✓ MARANDI *At Stelida, tel. (0285) 24652, 24784, (01) 2026984, fax (0285) 24652.* Small, charming, with pool and a fine location on the beach, next to Naxos Beach II. **Price: 25,000-50,000 drs.** (€ 73.37-146.74)

✓ KAVOS *At Agios Prokopis, tel. (0285) 23355, 23907, fax 23834.* Studios and villas on the hill above the beach. **Price: 15,000-45,000 drs.**(€ 44.02-132.06)

✓ HOTEL PROTEAS
At Agios Prokopis, tel. (0285) 26134, fax 23328. New hotel built in "island style" on the hill above the beach. Large rooms, with A/C, TV, telephone and mini bar. Good service, bar, safebox, lounge, foreign exchange, pool and facilities for people with special needs. **Price: 13,000-25,000 drs.**(€ 38.15-73.37)

SEMELI *At Agios Prokopis, tel. (0285) 41977.* Well-maintained, clean rooms, with A/C, TV and fridge, 400 m from the beach. A good choice for this price range. **Price: 16,000-22,000 drs.** (€ 46.96-64.56)

VILLA ADRIANA *On Stelida hill, tel. (0285) 42804.* Attractively decorated, attentive service, overlooking Agios Prokopis beach. **Price: 10,000-19,000 drs.** (€ 29.35-55.76)

ALTERNATIVES

HOTEL KAVOURAS VILLAGE *Tel. (0285) 23705, 25580, fax 25802.* Large hotel-bungalow complex on the beach at Agios Prokopis. Rooms with TV and telephone. Also bar, restaurant, parking, tennis court, playground, pool and bus service. **Price: 15,000-42,000 drs.** (€ 44.02-132.26)

BIRIKOS *Tel. (0285) 25474, fax 41654.* Small apartments at Agios Prokopis, with pool. **Price: 6,000-16,000 drs.** (€ 17.61-46.96)

AGIA ANNA

✓ HOTEL IRIA BEACH (C Class)
Agia Anna beach, tel. (0285) 42600-2, fax 42603
Open: April-October. **Description:** Good location right on the beach. Built in traditional Cycladic style. **Rooms:** 28 spacious rooms, with kitchenette and balcony or veranda overlooking the sea. **Special features:** Restaurant, Zas Travel Bureau, for-

eign exchange, car rental agency. **Price:** 14,000-45,000 drs. (€ 41.09-132.06) without breakfast. **Value for money:** ✱ **Credit cards:** Visa, Mastercard.

ALTERNATIVES

KASTELLO *Tel. (0285) 23082.* On the beach, between Agios Prokopis and Agia Anna. 10 nice rooms. **Price:** 7,000-14,000 drs. (€ 20.54-41.09)

AGIA ANNA *Tel. (0285) 41870.* We recommend this for its superb location right on the beach and for its price. Simple rooms with balcony. **Price:** 5,500-12,000 drs. (€ 16.14-35.22)

CAMPING
MARAGAS *Tel. (0285) 24552, 22293.* At Agia Anna, 600 pitches with facilities, shops, etc. Open from May-October. **Price:** 1,200-1,800 drs. (€ 3.52-5.28) per person.

Iria Beach

PLAKA

✓✓ VILLA MEDUSA RESORT (A Class)
On Plaka beach, tel. (0285) 75555, (01) 8940447, (0932) 523727, fax 25387, (01) 7790165, fax (0285) 75500

Open: April-October. **Description:** Pretty, small hotel complex a few steps from the beach with a large, well-tended garden boasting palm trees and tropical plants. **Rooms:** 18 rooms furnished with antiques, ceiling fans, TV, music, telephone, fridge, hairdryer and seaview. **Special features:** Restaurant with BBQ, beach bar, mini bus to and from Hora, playground, pergola for breakfast, parking. Pets permitted by prior arrangement. **Price:** 28,000-42,000 drs. (€ 82.17-123.26), with breakfast. **Value for money:** ✱ ✱ ✱ **Credit cards:** All.

ANOTHER BEST SELECTION

3 ADELFIA *On Plaka beach, tel. (0285) 41347, 41571.* Quiet hotel in a superb location right on the sea. **Price:** Upon request.

MIKRI VIGLA - ORKOS

✓✓ HOTEL ORKOS VILLAGE (C Class)
Tel. (0285) 75321, (0932) 423568, fax (0285) 75320

Open: May-October. **Description:** A real find! This is a great place to stay. The Norwegian owner has designed a delightful little hotel on the hill above Orkos. Everything is simple and attractive, in traditional style both inside and out. You'll have a panoramic view and the sandy coves at your feet. **Rooms:** 26 pretty rooms, with built-in beds (doubles and singles), balcony, sitting room and kitchenette. **Special features:** Rock garden, breakfast on the veranda surrounded by a lovely flower-filled garden. Stunning view, taverna, bar and parking. Our only reservation, its many steps up from the road. **Price:** 14,000-27,000 drs. (€ 41.09-79.24). **Value for money:** ✱ ✱ ✱ **Credit cards:** None.

ANOTHER BEST SELECTION

✓ MIKRI VIGLA HOTEL BUNGALOWS *Near the beach at Mikri Vigla, tel. (0285) 75241, fax 75240.* Rooms with TV, telephone and mini bar. Taverna, bar, playground, pool, foreign exchange, free transport to and from port, windsurfing centre, parking. **Price:** 12,000-27,000 drs. (€ 35.22-79.24)

ALTERNATIVE

STUDIOS OASIS *Tel. (0285) 75494, fax 75337.* A rooms complex above the ordinary, attractive inside and out. With kitchen, telephone and TV. Pool, bar, cafe and parking. **Price:** 13,000-23,000 drs. (€ 38.15-67.50)

KASTRAKI

✓ SUMMERLAND COMPLEX (A Class)
Kastraki beach, tel. (0285)75461-2, fax 75339. Tastefully designed hotel complex in Cycladic style. The best in Kastraki, 250 m from the beach. With a beautiful garden, verandas, and peace and quiet, pleasant decor, pools, jacuzzi, gym, tennis court, playground, mini market, foreign exchange, parking and car/motorbike rental agency. **Price:** 16,150-26,900 drs. (€ 47.40-78.94)

ROMAZZA STUDIOS
Alyko beach, tel. (0285) 75230, 75025. New building in a beautiful, quiet spot on the beach, overlooking the sea. **Price:** Upon request.

PYRGAKI

✓ HOTEL FINIKAS
50 m from the beach, tel. (0285) 75230, fax 75025
Open: April-September. **Description:** New (in 1998) and well looked after, with a large garden and palm trees, right on the beach. Ideal for getting away from it all. **Rooms:** 10 immaculate studios, with kitchenette, fridge, satellite TV, radio telephone and hairdryer. **Special features:** Pool, attractive poolside bar and playground. Pets allowed on prearrangement. **Price:** Upon request. **Value for money:** ✱ ✱ ✱ **Credit cards:** None.

AGIASSOS

VRAHIA
Agiassos beach, tel. and fax (0285) 75533, 75053, (01) 8223823. 16 clean, good standard rooms, with a view. Garden and good taverna on the tranquil beach. **Price:** Upon request.

BEST RESTAURANTS
AND TAVERNAS

Naxos offers many fine possibilities for eating out. In the Hora there are lots of restaurants serving both international and Greek cuisine, while the inland villages and southwest beaches specialize in local meat dishes. Good fresh fish and lobster may be had at the fish tavernas around Moutsouna.

PRICES

For two persons with salad, main dish and the cheapest wine on the menu: € *up to 8,000 drs.* (23.48 euro), € € *from 8,000 to 16,000 drs.* (23.48-46.96 euro), € € € *over 16,000 drs.* (46.96 euro)

HORA - AGIOS GEORGIOS

✓✓ ELLI'S RESTAURANT

At Grotta, tel. (0285) 24476
Near the port, excellent international cuisine served in pleasant, attractive surroundings. **Price:** € €

✓✓ EL MIRADOR

At Grotta, tel. (0285) 22655
On the floor above Elli's, with a splendid veranda. Mexican food served to Latin rhythms. **Price:** € €

✓✓ PORTOKALI CLUB

On Agios Georgios bay.
Tel. (0285) 22375
In a spell-binding location on the cape with a stupendous view of the sea. Cafe-

bar-restaurant serving international cuisine in a particularly attractive setting (The second star is for the setting.)
Price: €

✓✓ THE OLD INN

In the Old Town, tel. (0285) 26093
In a narrow lane above the taxi stand. Attractive surroundings, with traditional decor, antiques shop, pretty garden and playground. German and international cooking. **Price:** € €

✓✓ LALOS-KARNAYIO

At the far end of the port.
Tel. (0285) 23057
Eccentric proprietor with a devoted following. Traditional Greek cooking and fresh fish. **Price:** €

✓ IL GIRASOLE

On the port, tel. (0285) 23326
Pizzeria-snacks in a good location with
good service. **Price:** €

✓ KASTRO

*At the south entrance to the Kastro.
Tel. (0285) 22005*
On Prandouna square. Lovely view of
the town and the sea, plus good Greek
cooking with traditional dishes.
Price: €

✓ APOLAFSIS

Above the port, tel. (0285) 22178
On a veranda with a view of the port.
Greek casseroles and fish dishes. Live
music every Friday and Saturday with
old Greek songs and a guitar accompa-
niment. **Price:** €

✓ VASILIS

In the Old Town, tel. (0285) 23763
Picturesque taverna in an Old Town al-
ley, with Greek cuisine and the best
moussaka in miles. **Price:** €

✓ KLIMATARIA

*Papavasiliou street
Tel. (0285) 22645, 23425*
Fine Greek cooking and grills, in a courtyard with a grape arbour and potted
plants. Quick service. **Price:** €

✓ LOUKOULLOS

In the Old Town, tel. (0285) 22569
Small, almost a dive, in a charming alleyway. Greek cooking, grills and attractive decor. **Price:** €

✓ AIGAION PELAGOS

*Behind Alpha Bank on a small enclosed
square, tel. (0285) 25885*
A cafe-restaurant with a difference. Live
music, delicious Greek appetizers
(mezedes) and local desserts.
Price: € €

✓ SCIROCCO

Plateia Protodikeiou, tel. (0285) 25931
Delicious mezedes, island atmosphere and good service in a busy area. The restaurant is famous for its fresh fish. **Price:** €

✓ KAVOURI

At Agios Georgios.
Tel. (0285) 23729, 23117
Old restaurant by the sea, Greek cuisine. **Price:** €

✓ MANOLIS GARDEN

In the Old Town, tel. (0285) 25168
The place may be small but it does have a garden, a rarity in the Old Town. Traditional Greek cooking and tasty appetizers. **Price:** € €

TO STEKI TOU VALETA

On the port, next to the Limanaki taverna, tel. (0285) 22235
Where the locals go for raki (Greece's grappa) and nibbles. **Price:** €

LIMANAKI

On the port, tel. (0285) 25332
Another favourite with the locals. Fish, grilled octopus and other treats.
Price: € €

CLASSICO

Overlooking the port, tel. (0285) 26106
Italian specialities and a wonderful view of Naxos harbour. Pleasant ambience and attractive decor. **Price:** €

NIKOS KATSAGANIS

On the waterfront, tel. (0285) 23153
One of the island's oldest eating places, it's reliable and the fish is fresh. One flight up, overlooking the port. **Price:** €

APEIRANTHOS

✓✓ LEFTERIS

Tel. (0285) 61333
Excellent pastry shop by day, wonderful home cooking in the evening. The veranda setting and view are particularly appealing. **Price:** €

✓ PLATANOS
Tel. (0285) 61460
"Chop house" in a superb location shaded by plane trees next to a tower-house. **Price:** €

INLAND

ANO POTAMIA

✓ PIGHI

In the village square, tel. (0285) 32292
Simple food in pretty surroundings, with a garden and the river nearby.
Price: €

BETWEEN HORA AND APOLLONAS

ENGARES

✓ HARIS
Tel. (0285) 62226
Family taverna with low prices in a tran-quil location, far from the madding tourists. **Price:** €

ABRAMI BAY

EFTHYMIOS

Tel. (0285) 63244
No-frills fish taverna in a prime location overlooking the pretty cove.
Price: €

SOUTHWEST COAST

AGIOS PROKOPIOS

✓✓ AVALI
On the hillside at Agios Prokopis, tel. (0285) 41971, (0944) 542695
Exceptional restaurant in a superb spot at the edge of the beach with a view all the way up it. Sophisticated menu, wide range of choices: fish and seafood, local specialities and produce, excellent service. **Price:** €

✓ SPYROS

On the beach at Agios Prokopis, tel. (0285) 42055
Good Greek cooking. One of the best in the resort. **Price:** €

✓ FOTIS

Tel. (0285) 42123
Greek cooking all year round.
Price: € €

AGIA ANNA

✓ FAROS

On the beach, tel. (0285) 24530, 24047
Classic fish taverna, fish soups and other delicacies. **Price:** €

✓ GORGONA

On the beach, tel. (0285) 41007
Quick service and lots of people in a picturesque spot next to where the fishing caiques tie up. **Price:** €

✓ BANANA (formerly ISLAND)
On the beach, tel. (0285) 41891
Nightclub which also serves decent food, specializing in Brazilian and international cuisine, accompanied by good music.
Price: €

✓ PARADISO

Just beyond Agia Anna, at Paradisos.
Tel. (0285) 42026
Greek cooking far from the masses.
Price: €

MIKRI VIGLA

✓ KONTOS

On the beach, tel. (0285) 75215
Wonderful location, pleasant ambience, Greek cuisine. **Price:** €

KASTRAKI

✓✓ AXIOTISSA
At the 18th km on the Hora-Alykos road.
Tel. (0285) 75107
Wonderful taverna, run by young people with enthusiasm and originality. Try the creative concoctions inspired by various places, Greek and foreign, from tabbouleh to pizza, and the full range of Naxos cheeses. Barrel wine, pergola. Open winter and summer, except November. **Price:** €

i
BEST TIPS AND INFORMATION

TRANSPORTATION

HOW TO GET THERE

By air from Athens: Regular Olympic Airways flights, 45 minutes. Information: OA Athens tel. (01) 9666666, OA Naxos tel. (0285) 23830, Naxos airport tel. (0285) 23292. *For information about the new Athens airport at Spata, ask your travel agent. Airport tel. (01) 3530000.*

By ferry: From Piraeus in 6 1/2 hours or from Rafina in 5 1/2 hours. Information Piraeus Port Authority tel. (01) 4226000-6, Piraeus booking agencies tel. (01) 4124800, 4177453, 4124900, 4119264, Rafina Port Authority tel. (0294) 22487, 28888, Naxos Port Police tel. (0285) 22300, 23840.

By high-speed catamaran: From Piraeus (Akti Tzelepi) in 3 hours 50 minutes or from Rafina in 3 hours 10 minutes. Information: Piraeus Port Authority tel. (01) 4226000-6, Piraeus booking agencies tel. (01) 4199000, 6164444, Rafina Port Authority tel. (0294) 22487, 28888, Naxos Port Police tel. (0285) 22300, 23840.

By hydrofoil (Flying Dolphin): From Rafina in 3 hours 15 minutes. Information: Rafina Port Authority tel. (0294) 22487, 28888.

Athens-Rafina: By public (KTEL) bus several times a day, departing from the Pedio tou Areos (Patissia), tel. (01) 8210872.

As we go to press, inter-island ferry schedules are in the process of being reorganized, and the smaller travel agents usually deal with only one of the shipping lines that serve the Aegean islands and don't tell you about other options. For a fuller picture, we suggest you use a large travel agent or look up the following Website: www.yen.gr Also, ticket prices will be increasing by 7 to 10%.

CONNECTIONS

Naxos is linked with most of the other Cyclades (Syros, Tinos, Mykonos, Paros, Amorgos, Donousa, Schinousa, Iraklia, Koufonissia, Ios, Sikinos, Folegandros, Santorini, Anafi), with the Eastern Aegean islands, the Dodecanese and Heraklion, Crete.
Information: Piraeus Port Authority tel. (01) 4226000-6, 4172657, 4511311. Rafina Port Authority tel. (0294) 22487, 28888, Naxos Port Authority tel. (0285) 22300.

HOW TO GET AROUND

The paved road network is in satisfactory condition, but the roads are apt to be winding and narrow; there are also a good number of acceptable unpaved roads. If you don't take your own car, we recommend you rent some form of transport from one of the many car and motorcycle agencies on the island.
Otherwise, you can get around using the **public bus system**. Regularly scheduled buses leave Hora for the island's larger villages and summer resorts (KTEL Naxos, tel. 0285 22291). The island has several taxis, based in Hora and the bigger villages (Hora, tel. 0285-22444, 24331 and Filoti tel. 31328). Hiring a taxi with a knowledgeable driver is perhaps the best way to see the churches and landmarks in the interior, if you want to avoid the hassle of discovering them on your own.

CAR AND SCOOTER RENTALS

NAXOS TOWN 0285

CarNET 24390
Motorbike Rentals-Billy Motor Power .... 25046, 42046 (AgiosProkopis)
Hertz 26600
Akrogiali Tours 22236
Funsea 22009
Moto Rent Sousounis 25765

IF YOU HAVE A BOAT

There is a yacht refuelling station in Naxos harbour, where water and repair service are also available. You can also tie up on the pier at Agia Anna, Alyko, Apollonas and Moutsouna. In Plaka bay there's a rock called Aspronissi and at Orkos, the next bay, is another rock, Parthena, with a chapel dedicated to the Panagia Parthena, favourite bathing spots for yachtspeople with snorkels. If you're thinking of sailing round the island, don't forget that Naxos is large with **148** kilometres of coast line and the north winds (meltemia) can make the north and east coasts quite disagreeable.

BEST TIPS

BEST ENTERTAINMENT

In Hora: Entertainment on Naxos is concentrated on the waterfront, where you'll find a wide gamut of cafes and pocket-size bars. We like √ √ **Musique Caffe** and √ √ **Musique Connection**, with good music, great breakfasts, fruit juices and coffee throughout the day. Later drop by the √ √ **Ocean Club**, where the "kefi" (Greek high spirits) and music don't cease until the sun comes up. Other fun places are √ **Veggera** and √ **Cream**, a new hangout at the end of the waterfront, and don't forget to check the action at **Jam** and **Ecstasis**.

In the Old Town: One of the island's oldest and most popular bars is √ √ **Fragile** while the √ √ **Jazz Bar Lakridi** on Palias Agoras street is a newer favourite.

Veggera

Cream

Jazz Bar Lakridi

Kahlua

√ **Super Island** and √ **Day & Night** are in with visiting Athenians, while the classic √ **Sante** bar has a beautiful terrace for sitting and admiring the view of Naxos by night. **Kasuma** and **Sanoudos** are other good choices.

At Agios Georgios: Things are hopping at √ √ **Portokali**, just outside Hora on the cape with a fine view, and at √ **La Plaza Cafe** on the most crowded part of the beach.

At Agios Prokopis: For music and a party atmosphere both day and night, try **Kahlua**, right on the sea.

At Agia Anna: Here you'll find the waterfront nightclub √ **Banana** (formerly Island), **Seven Club** and the cafe-bar **Aigaio Pelagos**, where you can listen to Greek blues (rebetika). Want to sample a traditional Greek club with singers, musicians, dancing and whisky? The biggest bouzouki establishment is **Enosi**, near the little port.

BEST SEASON

Easter Week, May, June and September are the best months for visiting Naxos. In July and August the island is virtually flooded with tourists, Greek and foreign, but if that's your choice then be sure to secure a room, preferably in one of the resorts on the southwest coast or Moutsouna and avoid Hora.

BEST BUYS

Spoon sweets (preserves), local cheeses and traditional *kitro* liqueurs made from citrus fruit with the Valindra label can all be bought in the Old Town at Takis Shop. Pretty hand-made ceramics and olive-wood products at L'Olivier in Halki.

BEST LOCAL FOOD

Naxos produces excellent meats, vegetables and cheeses, such as *arseniko* (hard goat cheese) and *thiliko* (fresh cheese), *xinomyzithra* (a crumbly semi-fresh cheese), *graviera* (like gruyere) and *kopanisti* (a fermented piquant soft cheese). Try the scrumptious Naxos fries (chips) — Naxos potatoes are famous — and when in the interior ask for game (wild rabbit or partridge) in the autumn. Other island specialities are *patsas* (tripe soup), good for hangovers, and *batoudo*, eaten at Easter.

As on most of the Cyclades, where water shortages are common, we recommend you drink bottled water.

WEATHER CHART

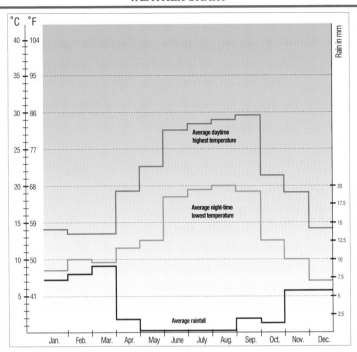

From end July and throughout August, as in all the Cyclades islands, northerly winds, known as meltemia, blow strongly. Although they have a blessedly cooling effect they can be a hazard to boats out at sea and tricky for swimmers too, to the extent that some of the more exposed beaches can be practically unusable.

INFORMATION

TICKET AND TRAVEL AGENTS

BANKS

Alpha Bank .... (0285) 22996
National Bank .... (0285) 25895
Commercial Bank .... (0285) 23055
Ioniki - Piraeus Bank .... (0285) 26100
Eurobank - Ergasias .... (0285) 26025
Agricultural Bank... (0285) 22818

USEFUL TELEPHONE NUMBERS

NAXOS 0285
Naxos Tourist Information Centre
.........22993, 24525, 25201, 26123
Town Hall.................21361, 22717
Police 22100, 23280
Public Buses (KTEL) 22291
Port Police............................ 22300
Taxis 22444
Health Centre
.....................23333, 23550, 23676
Newstand-Foreign Press....... 23675

APEIRANTHOS 0285
Police.................................... 61211
Clinic 61206

MELANES......................... 0285
Clinic 62372

HALKI 0285
Police.................................... 31224
Clinic 31206
Pharmacy 31218

FILOTI 0285
Taxis 31328
Clinic 31204
Pharmacy 31787

BIBLIOGRAPHY

Istoria tou Ellinikou Ethnous, Ekdotike Athenon, Athens.

Potamianou Aheimastou, Myrtali, *Elliniki Techni: Vyzantines Tihografies*, Ekdotike Athenon, Athens.

Les Merveilles des Musées Grecs, Ekdotike Athenon, Athens.

Katsouros, K., *Naxos: The flower of the East,* Istorikos Omilos Naxou

Zafiropoulou, Fotini, *Naxos: Mnimeia kai Mouseia,* Krini, Athens, 1988.

Ucke, Christian & M. Hofbauer, *Walking Tours on Naxos*, P.H. Verlag.

Naxos: Byzantine Art in Greece, Melissa, 1989.

INDEX

A

B

C

D

E

F

H

I

K

INDEX

"An eruption" of flavour and aroma ...

(Boutari Assyrtiko from Santorini)

The thick evening mist gives to the vines the precious moisture. The volcanic soil offers its unique elements. High temperature, strong winds and rare rainfalls; exceptional conditions that contribute to ideal grape maturity. A wine of golden colour, subtle aroma, full body and strong personality. Boutari Assyrtiko. From Santorini.

BOUTARI
FOURTH GENERATION

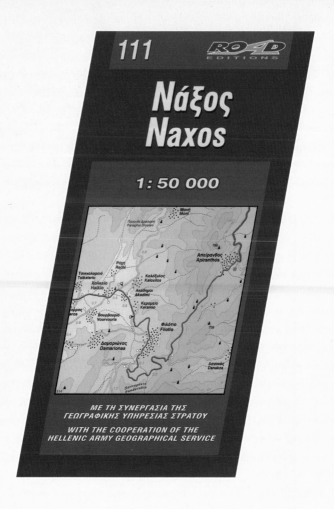

Only the Best
recommend
the *ROAD* map
of Naxos

Information, tel.: (01) 3640723

visit www.greeceonlythebest.gr